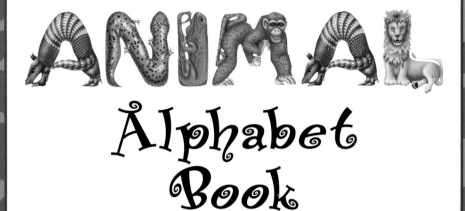

ANIMAL

Alphabet
Book

written and illustrated by
Donna Kern

COVE
PRESS

An imprint of
U.S. GAMES SYSTEMS, INC.
179 Ludlow Street
Stamford, CT 06902 USA

A is for Armadillo
adorned with a shell,
encased in full armor,
right down to his tail.

B

B is for Bear
in a national park,
eating bumblebee honey,
bugs, berries, and bark.

C is for Cat
the most cunning of creatures,
a cute, cozy pet,
with cuddly features.

D is for Dogs
a Dachshund duet,
these dogs are delightful,
dependable pets.

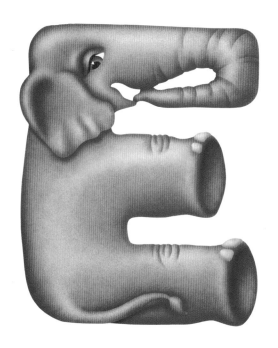

E is for Elephant
enormous yet elegant,
everyone knows
he's extremely intelligent.

F is for Frog
he's frightfully fond
of feasting on food
like the flies in his pond.

G is for Giraffe
graceful and grand,
a gentle giant
who'll eat from your hand.

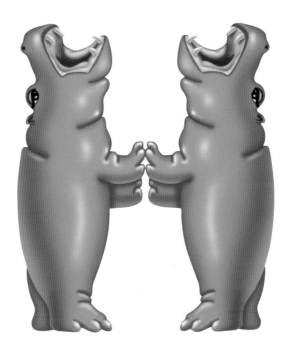

H is for Hippos
who inhabit the hollow
and retreat from the heat
in the mud where they wallow.

I is for Iguana
an incredible lizard,
who runs very fast,
and disappears like a wizard.

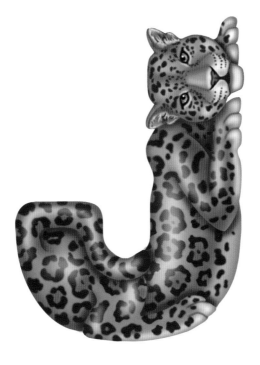

J is for Jaguar
he is justly proud
to joyfully joust with
the whole jungle crowd.

K is for Kangaroo
with kick-boxing feet,
he's king of the ring
and always upbeat.

L is for Lion
with his long, luscious mane,
he's the legendary lord
of his domain.

M is for Monkey
they mimic and mime,
and muster up mischief
most of the time.

N is for Newt
they're normally seen
where it's dark and shady
and leafy and green.

O is for Otter
a swimmer who's bold,
the oil in his fur
protects him from cold.

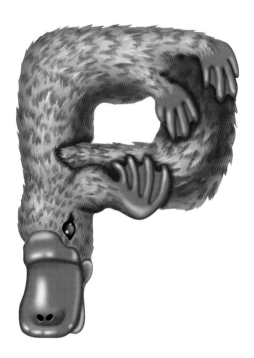

P is for Platypus
who has a duck's bill,
his webbed feet are part
of his playful appeal.

Q is for Quail
flying quickly until
he hides in the brush,
very quiet and still.

R is for Raccoon
they don't mean to be rude,
they're rascals who rummage
through rubbish for food.

S is for Seal
he can swim on his back,
or show off and do stunts
for a small sardine snack.

T is for Tiger
who treads on the trail,
truly terrific
from his tip to his tail.

U is for Unicorn
a most unusual sight,
an utterly unique
and unearthly delight.

V is for Vulture
who keeps vigil all day,
voraciously waiting
for vulnerable prey.

W is for Weasel
he's wily and bright,
waiting for winter
when he will turn white.

X is for eXtinct
as X-rays will show,
some fossils exist
from a long time ago.

Y is for Yak
much bigger than you,
you'll find him on mountains,
enjoying the view.

Z is for Zebra
in the zoo of course,
he's zippy and zany,
but not a striped horse!

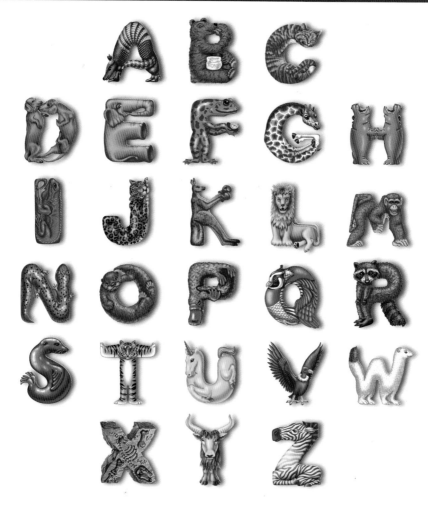

And so with animals you've filled your head,
from A to Z...now off to bed!